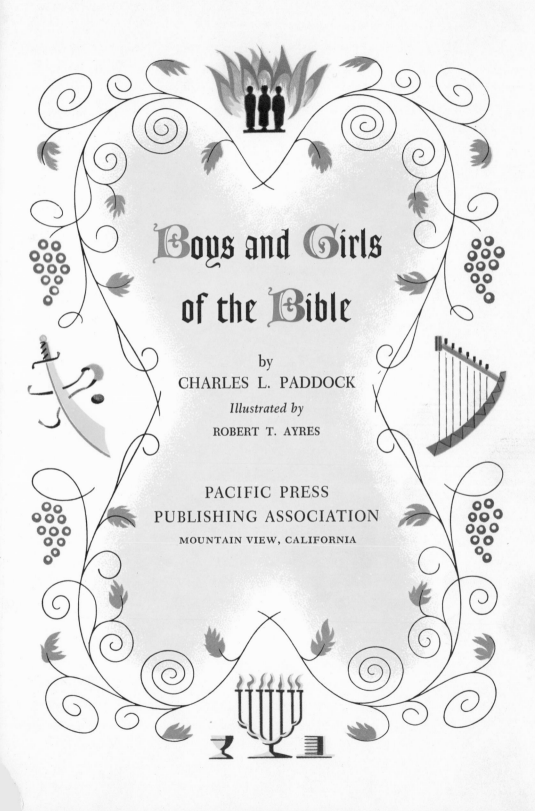

Boys and Girls

of the Bible

by

CHARLES L. PADDOCK

Illustrated by

ROBERT T. AYRES

PACIFIC PRESS
PUBLISHING ASSOCIATION
MOUNTAIN VIEW, CALIFORNIA

PACIFIC
PRESS
PUB.
ASSN.

OFFSET
IN U.S.A.

Presented to

Michael

by great Gradra Gartlly

with love and best wishes

A LITTLE MAIDEN
AND HER MASTER

AAMAN WAS A CAPTAIN in the army of a king. One day the army marched into the land of Israel and took many people prisoners. Naaman, the captain, took a little girl to work in his home. The army took her away from her father and her mother, and made her go to a strange land. She lived in the home of Naaman. She helped Naaman's wife wash the dishes, make the beds, and sweep the floor. This good little girl knew how to work. In her home she had been taught to love God and to pray

to Him. She was kind and happy, even when she was far from home.

Naaman, the captain, was a brave man. The king liked Naaman very much. But Naaman was very sick. The little girl felt sorry for him.

The little girl told Naaman's wife that there was a prophet in Israel who could cure Naaman. She wished Naaman could go to see this prophet and talk to him, so that Naaman could be well again.

Naaman heard the little girl's story, and he believed what she said. He went to Israel to find this prophet. He took gold and silver and some fine cloth with him, to give to the king of Israel.

The king could not help Naaman get well, but he knew Elisha, the man of God, who helped people. Elisha invited Naaman to come to his house.

Naaman, the captain of the army, went to see Elisha. The man of God told Naaman to go and wash in the Jordan River. He was to plunge into the water seven times, and then he would be well again.

Naaman did not want to go to the Jordan River. He did not think that going to the river would make him well. Besides, he knew there were bigger and better rivers in his own country. So he started toward home.

The soldiers of Naaman begged him to go down to the Jordan River and plunge in seven times, as Elisha, the man of God, had told him to do.

But Naaman said, "Why should I wash in that dirty little river? Elisha should wave his hands over me to heal me. But he didn't even come out to see me. He only sent word by a servant."

The soldiers said, "If Elisha asked you to do some big thing, you would do it. Why can't you do this little thing, when it may cure your sickness?"

At last Naaman decided to do as he was told. He plunged into the water. The soldiers counted: One, two, three, four, five, six, seven times! When Naaman came out of the water the last time he was well. His sickness had left him.

Naaman went back to the house of Elisha. He was so happy he wanted to thank Elisha. He knew that God had made him well. He wanted to give Elisha a gift, but Elisha would not take it. Elisha was happy to be of help to the captain of the army.

Naaman went back home a well man. He was thankful to the little maiden in his home. She believed in God, and she knew that God would make her master well.

Don't you imagine that Naaman gave the little girl a big hug? Don't you think he told her how happy he was that she believed in God, who heals people?

Read the story in 2 Kings 5.

SOLD AS A SLAVE

JACOB HAD TWELVE BOYS, and he loved each one. He loved Joseph more than any of his other sons. The father made a coat of many pretty colors for Joseph. The brothers of Joseph were angry. They did not want their father to love Joseph more than he loved them.

Joseph had two dreams, and he told these dreams to his brothers. In each dream his brothers bowed down to Joseph. When Joseph told his dreams, his brothers became more angry.

One time the brothers were a long way from home, taking care of their father's sheep. Jacob asked Joseph to go and see how the sons were. Joseph walked and walked, for it was more than fifty miles from home.

When his brothers saw Joseph coming, they said, "Here comes the dreamer." They wanted to get rid of Joseph. One of the boys was named Reuben. He said, "Let us not kill him, but cast him into this pit." He hoped he might get Joseph out of the pit when the brothers were not looking. He planned to send Joseph back to his father Jacob. Joseph was put down into a deep pit. The brothers took the coat of many pretty colors and dipped it in the blood of a goat. They took the coat home to their father and told him something must have happened to Joseph. Father Jacob was very sad, for he loved Joseph dearly.

The brothers took Joseph out of the pit and sent him to the faraway land of Egypt with some men. Joseph walked beside the camels as they made the trip over the hot desert. Joseph was sad as he said good-by to his brothers and looked across the fields and hills toward his home.

Joseph went to work in Egypt. He did his work well, and God was with him.

Although Joseph was honest and kind, someone told lies about him, and he was put in prison. Joseph was in prison for a long, long time, but he loved God and helped other men in the prison.

After many months in prison, Joseph was remembered by a friend. The king had a dream, and the friend of Joseph told the king that the man in prison could tell the king the meaning of his dream. The king sent for Joseph and told him of his dream. Joseph told the king there would be seven years when there would be plenty of food.

Then there would be seven years when the wheat would not grow and there would be little to eat. Joseph told the king to save food in the seven years of plenty and keep it for the years when people would be hungry.

The king gave Joseph the job of helping the nation. Joseph built barns and big store-houses, and he saved much food for the years when people would be hungry.

Back at the home of Joseph, the father and the brothers had no food. Father Jacob asked his sons to go to Egypt to get food for them to eat. Ten of the brothers went to Egypt to buy food.

The youngest brother, named Benjamin, did not go. The brothers came to Joseph to buy food. Joseph knew they were his brothers, but they did not know him. They bowed down to him, as he had seen them do in his dreams many years before.

Joseph was very kind to his brothers,

and he asked about his father and his brother Benjamin. Joseph asked the brothers to go home and bring Benjamin to Egypt. They were sure father Jacob would not let Benjamin come. Joseph put the brothers in prison for three days. Then Joseph told them they would have to leave one of the brothers in Egypt while the other nine took food home. The brothers must come back and bring Benjamin with them.

When the food was gone, father Jacob told his sons to go back to Egypt to buy more to eat. They took Benjamin with them. When all the brothers were in the room together, Joseph told them he was their brother. He sent them home to bring Jacob and all his loved ones to Egypt.

Father Jacob and his sons and their families came to Egypt to live. Joseph rode to meet them. Father Jacob put his arms around Joseph. How happy he was to see his son again!

Joseph loved and obeyed God, and the Lord had been good to him through all the years.

Read the story in Genesis 37-47.

THE BOY SAMUEL

HANNAH WAS A KIND woman who loved boys and girls. She prayed to God that she might have a son. The loving God answered her prayer, and a son was born in the home. Hannah and her husband were happy.

The boy was named Samuel. Hannah loved Samuel very much, and she taught him to love and obey God.

Hannah and her husband went up to the temple to worship God. They took the boy Samuel with them. Hannah told the priest that God had answered her prayer and given her this boy. Now she wanted him to serve God in the temple.

Hannah went home and left Samuel at the temple so that he could learn to work for God. Every day Hannah prayed for Samuel. Each year when she went to the temple she took Samuel a pretty coat she had made for him. She was happy that Samuel worked for God.

Samuel was busy helping in the temple. He was very careful to do good work.

One night when Samuel was asleep in his bed, he thought he heard someone call, "Samuel!" He jumped out of bed and ran to the room of the priest. He said, "Here am I." Eli told Samuel he had not called him, and that he should go back to bed and go to sleep.

Samuel heard the voice again, and he once more jumped out of his bed and ran to Eli. He told the priest he had surely called for Samuel. Eli had not called the boy and told him to go back to bed again. Then the Lord called Samuel the third time. Samuel ran into Eli's room again and said he must have called him.

Eli knew the Lord was calling the boy and told him to go back to bed, and if he heard the voice once more he should say, "Speak, Lord, for Thy servant heareth."

The Lord talked with Samuel, and when he grew up he was a good leader for God and helped his people.

The Bible says, too, that "Samuel grew, and the Lord was with him." The boy grew up to be a man, a good man, and did a great work for God. God has a work for every boy and girl to do.

Read the story in 1 Samuel 1-3.

MOSES IN A BASKET

A BABY NAMED MOSES was born to a happy father and mother. But they were made sad, for the wicked king was going to take all the little boys from their fathers and mothers. The mother of Moses did not want the king to find him, so she decided to hide him where he could not be found. Where could she hide baby Moses so that he would be safe? She made a basket big enough to hold the baby. She lined the basket with soft cloth. The outside of the basket she covered with paint so it would float on the water and the baby would not get wet. The

basket must have had a cover on it so the hot sun would not shine in the baby's eyes.

When no one was watching, the mother of Moses put her baby in the basket and set it to float on the river among the tall grass. The tall grass hid the basket and kept it close to the shore. The mother of Moses hoped and prayed that the baby would be safe.

Now, Miriam was the sister of Moses. She loved her little brother. When baby Moses was put in the basket, Miriam played by the riverbank, so she could watch the basket boat. Most girls like to care for their little brothers and sisters.

One morning the king's daughter came down to the river to bathe. She had her servants with her. As she walked out into the water, the woman saw the basket and had a servant bring it to her. When the cover was taken off the basket, there was baby Moses.

Then Miriam ran quickly to the king's daughter and asked if she should go and find someone to care for the baby. The king's daughter said Yes, so Miriam ran and got her mother.

The mother of Moses came to see the daughter of the king. Baby Moses was given to his mother by the daughter of the king. You may be sure the mother took good care of her baby.

The mother of Moses cared for him until he was twelve years old. His sister Miriam helped to care for him, too. The mother of Moses taught him to love God and to be a good boy. When Moses was twelve years old, he went to live in the palace with the daughter of the king. Moses became a strong leader who saved his people. God blessed Moses in all his work.

Read the story in Exodus 2:1-10.

THE BOY AND
THE GIANT

IN BETHLEHEM LIVED A BOY named David. Because he was a small boy he cared for the sheep of Jesse, his father. David led the sheep to the green hills, where he sang songs and played on his harp.

David loved God, and he wanted to help others. He watched the stars shine in the night sky.

One day the good man Samuel was told to go to Bethlehem and bless one of the sons of Jesse, for God wanted this son to be king. Samuel went to the home of Jesse. Samuel asked for the tall, strong son, whose

name was Eliab. He was the oldest son, with bright eyes and rosy red cheeks. God told Samuel this was not the son to be king. God does not look on our clothes or pretty face; He looks at our heart. God wants us to be good and kind and loving.

Six more boys came before Samuel, but none of these was to be king. Samuel asked Jesse if he had any more sons. The father said he had one more boy named David, who was caring for the sheep. They sent for David to come from the hills to see Samuel.

The Lord told Samuel, "This is he." This was the boy who was to be king. David went back to the quiet hills to care for the sheep, to play on his harp, and to sing songs of praise to God. It was not yet time for David to be king.

The army was at war. Three of David's brothers had gone to the army. Jesse asked David to take some food to his three brothers in the army. When David came near to the camp where the soldiers were, he heard a great noise. The enemy had a big, strong giant, named Goliath, who marched out and dared any of the soldiers to come and fight with him. The soldiers were all afraid of the giant.

David was not afraid, for he knew God was with him. David said that God had helped him to kill a lion and a bear that came after his sheep.

David said, "I will go and fight." He was not afraid of the giant.

David went out to meet the giant Goliath with only a sling. From the brook David picked up five smooth, round stones to put in his sling.

Giant Goliath saw David coming out to meet him, and he made fun of him. David was not afraid. He said to giant Goliath, "I come in the name of the Lord." David knew that God was with him.

David put a stone in his sling and threw it with all his might. It hit Goliath in the middle of his forehead. Giant Goliath fell on his face. David had the victory over the giant, and the enemy soldiers ran away.

Read the story in 1 Samuel 16; 17.

A SICK
LITTLE GIRL

ONE DAY WHEN JESUS had sailed across the blue lake He found a crowd of people waiting for Him on the shore. Jesus talked to them and healed some of the sick. Then He went home to dinner with His friend Matthew.

While Jesus was eating dinner, a man came to see Him. Jesus went to see what the man wanted. Jairus, one of the leaders of the city, had come for help. He fell down at the feet of Jesus and begged Him to come to his home to see his little girl. She was so sick he was afraid she would die.

"Come and lay Thy hands on her," begged the father, "and she shall live." Jairus had faith to believe that Jesus would make his daughter well again.

Jesus wanted to help everyone, so He was happy to go with the man. The friends of Jesus also went with Him to the home of Jairus.

As they walked along the street, a woman pushed through the crowd and touched Jesus. She had been sick for many years and believed that she would be well if she could touch Jesus. Jesus saw the woman and said to her, "Daughter, thy faith hath made thee whole; go in peace." Jesus healed her, and she went away happy and strong.

Jairus, the father of the little girl, wanted to hurry. He saw a man running toward them. When he came near he told the father that his little girl was dead. Jairus was sad, for he loved his little girl very much. But he thought that since she was dead there was no need for Jesus to go home with him. Jesus knew what Jairus was thinking.

"Be not afraid," He said, "only believe."

Then Jesus told all the people who were following Him not to come any further. He took only Peter, James, and John with Him as He went on to Jairus's home.

When they came to the house they found many people called "mourners," who were crying loudly. The people always cried aloud when someone died. Jesus was sorry to hear them act this way.

"Why make ye this ado, and weep?" He asked. "The damsel is not dead, but sleepeth." This is the way Jesus talked about people who would be made alive again. The mourners laughed at Him.

Jesus sent them all away and took the father and the mother and His three disciples into the little girl's room.

The little girl lay on the bed as if she were fast asleep. Jesus walked over to the bed and took the hand of the girl. In a quiet voice He spoke, "I say unto thee, arise."

The girl's eyes opened, and she smiled. She jumped up and threw her arms around her father and mother. She was alive and happy. Jesus had made her well again.

The father and mother were happy. It was hard for some of the people to believe that the little girl was alive and well. Soon they stopped their crying and were happy, too. The friends all went home and told the story of the girl who had been dead but was made alive by Jesus.

Read the story in Mark 5:22-43.

A BOY AND HIS LUNCH

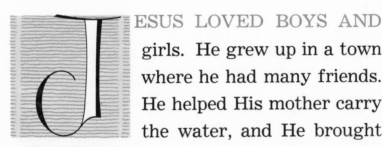

ESUS LOVED BOYS AND girls. He grew up in a town where he had many friends. He helped His mother carry the water, and He brought wood for the fire in the stove. When Jesus was a man, He helped the poor and cared for the sick. Many people wanted to see Him and to hear Him speak. He told many stories about flowers and birds and foxes. He made people well and brought happiness to those who were sad.

One day a little boy asked his mother if he could go over the hill with some of the other boys to see Jesus. His mother made him a lunch, and he put it in a basket. His mother must have told him to be a good boy as she kissed him good-by.

He must have been happy as he climbed the hill with the other boys, carrying his basket of lunch. Did you ever carry a lunch? I have. I used to take my lunch in a paper sack, in a pail, or in a basket. My mother made good lunches for me. While I walked along I sometimes peeked into the lunch to see what I had, and sometimes I ate part of my sandwiches before lunch-time. I think maybe this boy wanted to know what was in his lunch basket, and I wonder if he didn't lift up the lid and peek in. Do you know what was in his lunch basket? His mother knew what he liked to eat, and she had put in five barley buns and two fish.

After a while the boys reached the place where Jesus was speaking to a crowd of people. Do you know how many a thousand is? There were five thousand men there, and many women, and boys and girls, too.

Jesus made the sick well again, and He opened the eyes of the blind. He made lame people to walk. On this day He was telling stories, too. The little boy was having such a good time he forgot to eat his lunch.

It was late in the afternoon, and Jesus knew that the people had walked a long way. They were tired and hungry, but there were no stores or markets nearby. Jesus asked His friends if they had any food for the people. The friends of Jesus said there was not enough food to feed all these people. They said the people would have to go home and get something to eat.

Jesus asked if anyone in the crowd had any food. Someone said he had seen a boy with a lunch basket, and he might have some food in it.

The friends of Jesus brought this boy and his basket to Jesus. The boy opened his lunch basket, and there were five buns and two fish. Did Jesus want them?

That little boy was hungry, for he had walked a long way. Jesus asked him if he would give his lunch to feed the hungry people.

Some boys would have said, "No, sir; I am going to eat the buns and fish myself."

This boy thought of others. He was ready to give the lunch to Jesus. Jesus was going to give the food to other hungry boys and girls. The little boy must have watched Jesus bless the five buns and the two fish.

Something wonderful happened. Soon there were piles of buns and lots of dried fish. Jesus told the people to sit down in groups. Then the disciples filled baskets with the buns and the fish, and the people had plenty to eat.

I am sure the little boy had all he could eat, too. I think he ate and ate until he was no longer hungry. He did not lose anything by giving his lunch, did he?

As the sunset and night came, the people went home. The little boy ran part of the way home, I am sure, for he wanted to tell his mother what Jesus had said and done. How big his eyes must have been when he told his mother about Jesus. The good Man had fed thousands of people with the five buns and the two fish.

The boy's mother told him he was a good boy to give his lunch to Jesus. The boy knew he would never be sorry for giving to others.

Don't you wish you had been there that day? There were many boys and girls there. You would have seen Jesus. You would have seen Jesus heal the sick and make the blind people see again. You could have been right up close to Jesus, who loves you.

If you had been there that day with your lunch and had been very hungry, what would you have said to Jesus? If He had said, "Will you let me have your lunch, so that I can feed all these hungry people?" would you have said "Yes"? I am sure you would have. And you would have gone home happy.

Jesus gives us many good things. He wants us to share these good things with others. It makes us happy to give to others.

Read the story in Mark the sixth chapter and in Luke the ninth chapter.

THREE BOYS IN A FIERY FURNACE

MANY YEARS BEFORE Jesus was born, a king with a long name, Nebuchadnezzar, sent his soldiers to capture a city. The soldiers took some of the big boys from their homes to a city far away. The soldiers took strong boys who had clear eyes and rosy cheeks. King Nebuchadnezzar wanted to train these boys to be leaders in his country.

Three of these boys were Shadrach, Meshach, and Abednego. King Nebuchadnezzar was good to the boys, and he gave them a nice place to live. He gave them plenty

of food to eat and good clothes to wear.

King Nebuchadnezzar made a big gold statue, taller than a house. The king told all the people in the country to come and see this gold image. A band with horns and drums played music. The king told the people to bow before the gold statue.

King Nebuchadnezzar looked out over the crowd of people and he saw some who were not kneeling. The three boys, Shadrach, Meshach, and Abednego, did not bow to the gold image. The king told the boys to bow or he would put them in a hot furnace of fire.

Shadrach, Meshach, and Abednego loved God, and they prayed to Him. They did not bow before idols or statues. The three brave boys told the king they would not bow down to his gold statue. They would worship the true God.

King Nebuchadnezzar was very angry, and he told his soldiers to tie the hands and feet of Shadrach, Meshach, and Abednego. The furnace of fire was made seven times as hot as usual, and then the three brave boys were thrown into the fire. The fire was so hot that it burned the men to death who threw the boys into the furnace.

The king looked into the furnace to see the boys. Suddenly King Nebuchadnezzar shouted, for he saw the boys walking around in the furnace. The ropes that tied their hands and feet had burned off, but the boys were not hurt. The king looked again. Now he saw four persons in the furnace. Who could this fourth man be? The king said it looked like the Son of man. God had sent Him from heaven to protect Shadrach, Meshach, and Abednego, who were true to Him.

The king called to the three brave boys. He asked them to come out of the furnace of fire. The big boys walked out and talked to the king. Shadrach, Meshach, and Abednego told the king that God had cared for them, and that was why the fire did not hurt them at all. Their hair was not burned, and their clothes did not even smell of fire.

Don't you think these boys were happy that they had obeyed God and that God loved and cared for them?

King Nebuchadnezzar told all the people how God had saved the three brave boys from the furnace of fire.

Read the story in Daniel 3.

DANIEL IN THE LIONS' DEN

DANIEL WAS A BIG BOY almost full grown, when king Nebuchadnezzar and his soldiers came to the city. The soldiers marched through the streets. They went into the big church and took the dishes and pitchers of gold. They went to the homes of the people and took anything they wanted. The soldiers took Daniel with them to serve King Nebuchadnezzar. He went with the three brave boys, Shadrach, Meshach, and Abednego.

King Nebuchadnezzar wanted Daniel to work for him. He sent Daniel to school and gave him nice clothes and good food. Daniel loved God, and he was good and kind to others. Every morning, noon, and again at night, before he went to bed, Daniel knelt and prayed to God.

Daniel and the three brave boys did not want to eat some of the food the king gave them. It was not good for them to eat. Daniel asked for simple food. The servant of the king let the boys eat the kind of food they wanted. For ten days they ate simple food, and at the end of the ten days the boys had rosy cheeks and clear eyes. They were strong and they felt good.

Daniel helped King Nebuchadnezzar. He worked in the palace and became a leader.

After many years another king ruled the country. Daniel helped this king, too. Some of the people who worked for the king did not like Daniel. They said they must get rid of Daniel.

The people of this country bowed to idols

and statues, but Daniel prayed to God. Daniel knelt in prayer each morning, and noon, and at night before he went to bed.

The men in the palace who did not like Daniel asked the king to make a law that everyone must pray only to the king. The king made the law, and anyone who prayed to God, who made the world, would be put in a den with fierce lions. The men who did not like Daniel thought he would have to go into the den with the lions.

Daniel heard about the law, but he did not quit praying. He prayed in the morning, and at noon, and again at night. He prayed by his open window, where the men who did not like him could see him praying.

When the men saw Daniel praying, they ran to tell the king. They told the king that Daniel was breaking the law. He was praying to God who made the world; he did not pray to the king.

The king was sad, for he loved Daniel.

The men who did not like Daniel waited for the king to put his friend into the den with the lions. The soldiers of the king took Daniel to the den of fierce lions. There must have been five or ten or even more hungry lions. The soldiers who put Daniel in the den of lions were sure these big lions would eat Daniel.

That night the king could not sleep. He walked back and forth in his bedroom, for he thought of his friend Daniel.

Early in the morning the king hurried to the den of lions. He called Daniel, and Daniel answered. He was alive! The king saw Daniel walking around in the den with the lions. The fierce lions were gentle when Daniel was in the den. Daniel was happy to see the king. He told the king that God had sent an angel to be with him to keep the lions from hurting him.

The king was very happy to know that the lions had not hurt his friend Daniel.

The king said Daniel's God was the true God. The king told all his people to pray to Daniel's God. God loved Daniel, and He heard his prayers. Daniel's God is the God we pray to today. He loves all His children. He loves every boy and girl. He wants us to pray to Him. He hears our prayers, too.

Read the story in Daniel 6.

THE GIRL QUEEN

IN A LAND FAR ACROSS THE sea lived a rich king in a big palace. The king's palace had many rooms. Around the castle was a yard with green grass, tall trees, and pretty flowers. The king had servants to care for his gardens, to keep his horses, and to cook his food. The rich king had a long name. It was Ahasuerus.

Now, in the palace there was a beautiful queen named Vashti. She lived with King Ahasuerus. One time the king asked many friends to come to the palace. He told his servants to hang green and white and blue curtains around the yard. The servants put gold dishes on the table. There were many good things on the table. The friends came to the palace to eat with the king, and they stayed for many days.

Queen Vashti was not at the king's table because she was giving dinners for the wives of the king's friends. On the seventh day of the feast King Ahasuerus was having a merry time eating and drinking with his friends, when he thought it would be fun to have them all see the queen. So he sent seven of his best men to bring her before his friends to show off her beauty.

Vashti did not want to go before all those men. She sent back word to the king that she would not come. He was so angry that he asked the seven princes of the kingdom to tell him what to do to Vashti.

They said that Vashti had set a bad example before all the wives in the kingdom and that she should not be queen any more. Ahasuerus was pleased.

The king wanted to find another queen, and he sent his servants to search for a pretty girl. The servants found many pretty girls, and they were brought to the king's palace.

The king saw each of the girls, and he chose the girl he liked best to be his queen. The name of the girl was Esther, and she lived with her cousin.

Esther went to the palace to live. She had maids to make her pretty dresses. Queen Esther helped the king, and the king loved her.

There was a friend of the king who did not like Esther. He did not like the cousin of Esther or her people. This wicked man asked the king to pass a law that would destroy the people of the queen. The king signed the law, and many people were sad. The cousin of Esther heard about this law. He told Queen Esther she must ask the king to save her people.

The king had not sent for Queen Esther for many days. The queen prayed to God every day, and she asked God to help her see the king.

Esther took a bath and combed her hair. She put on a pretty dress and lovely slippers. She put the gold crown on her head. Then she went in to see King Ahasuerus. When the king saw her he smiled and told her he was glad to see her. He asked her why she had come to see him. Esther told the king that he had made a law that would hurt her people. She told him of her kind cousin who had once saved the king's life.

The king was happy to save the people of the queen. He told her that she did not need to worry any more, for he loved her dearly. The king saved the people of Queen Esther. So the queen and her cousin and their people were happy, all because Esther loved and obeyed God.

Read the story in the book of Esther.

The Ten Commandments

1. Thou shalt have no other gods before Me.
2. Thou shalt not make unto thee any graven image, or any likeness of anything that is in heaven above, or that is in the earth beneath, or that is in the water under the earth: thou shalt not bow down thyself to them, nor serve them: for I the Lord thy God am a jealous God, visiting the iniquity of the fathers upon the children unto the third and fourth generation of them that hate Me; and showing mercy unto thousands of them that love Me, and keep My commandments.
3. Thou shalt not take the name of the Lord thy God in vain; for the Lord will not hold him guiltless that taketh His name in vain.
4. Remember the Sabbath day, to keep it holy. Six days shalt thou labor, and do all thy work: but the seventh day is the Sabbath of the Lord thy God: in it thou shalt not do any work, thou, nor thy son, nor thy daughter, thy manservant, nor thy maidservant, nor thy cattle, nor thy stranger that is within thy gates: for in six days the Lord made heaven and earth, the sea, and all that in them is, and rested the seventh day: wherefore the Lord blessed the Sabbath day, and hallowed it.
5. Honor thy father and thy mother: that thy days may be long upon the land which the Lord thy God giveth thee.
6. Thou shalt not kill.
7. Thou shalt not commit adultery.
8. Thou shalt not steal.
9. Thou shalt not bear false witness against thy neighbor.
10. Thou shalt not covet thy neighbor's house, thou shalt not covet thy neighbor's wife, nor his manservant, nor his maidservant, nor his ox, nor his ass, nor anything that is thy neighbor's. *Exodus 20:3-17.*

JOE MANISCALCO